Birman Cats

by Connie Colwell Miller

Consulting Editor: Gail Saunders-Smith, PhD

Consultant: Jennifer Zablotny, DVM
Member, American Veterinary Medical Association

Capstone
press®

Mankato, Minnesota

Pebble Books are published by Capstone Press,
151 Good Counsel Drive, P.O. Box 669, Mankato, Minnesota 56002.
www.capstonepress.com

032010
5652VMI

Library of Congress Cataloging-in-Publication Data
Miller, Connie Colwell, 1976–
    Birman cats / by Connie Colwell Miller.
    p. cm. — (Pebble books. Cats)
    Includes bibliographical references and index.
    Summary: "Simple text and photographs present an introduction to the
Birman breed, its growth from kitten to adult, and pet care information" — Provided
by publisher.
    ISBN-13: 978-1-4296-1990-5 (hardcover)
    ISBN-10: 1-4296-1990-2 (hardcover)
    1. Birman cat — Juvenile literature. I. Title.
SF449.B5M44 2009
636.8'24 — dc22
                                                       2007051271

Note to Parents and Teachers

The Cats set supports national science standards related to life
science. This book describes and illustrates Birman cats. The images
support early readers in understanding the text. The repetition of
words and phrases helps early readers learn new words. This book
also introduces early readers to subject-specific vocabulary words,
which are defined in the Glossary section. Early readers may need
assistance to read some words and to use the Table of Contents,
Glossary, Read More, Internet Sites, and Index sections of the book.

Table of Contents

4

Beautiful Cats

Birmans are
beautiful cats.
Their shiny coats have
a light golden look.

Birmans' coats can be
many light colors.

Birmans have dark fur
on their faces, ears,
legs, and tails.
All Birmans have
bright white feet.

From Kitten to Adult

Birman kittens are born with round blue eyes. Their eyes stay blue as they grow.

Growing Birman kittens
are playful.
People say they act
like puppies.

Birmans are
fully grown
in three years.
Birmans are
medium-sized cats.

Caring for Birmans

Birmans' coats are silky. They should be brushed twice each week.

Birmans need
food and water
every day.

Birmans are beautiful
and friendly cats.
They make great pets.

Glossary

beautiful — very pleasant to look at

coat — an animal's hair or fur

friendly — helpful and kind

silky — very soft and smooth like silk

Read More

Barnes, Julia. *Pet Cats.* Pet Pals. Milwaukee: Gareth Stevens, 2007.

Shores, Erika L. *Caring for Your Cat.* Postively Pets. Mankato, Minn.: Capstone Press, 2007.

Internet Sites

FactHound offers a safe, fun way to find Internet sites related to this book. All of the sites on FactHound have been researched by our staff.

Here's how:

1. Visit *www.facthound.com*

2. Choose your grade level.

3. Type in this book ID **1429619902** for age-appropriate sites. You may also browse subjects by clicking on letters, or by clicking on pictures and words.

4. Click on the **Fetch It** button.

FactHound will fetch the best sites for you!

Index

Word Count: 102
Grade: 1
Early-Intervention Level: 12

Editorial Credits
Lori Shores, editor; Renée T. Doyle, set designer; Danielle Ceminsky, book designer;
   Wanda Winch, photo researcher

Photo Credits
Alamy/David Kilpatrick, 4
Can Stock Photo/bdenoon, 1, 22
Getty Images Inc./Altrendo Images, 20;
     Dorling Kindersley/Dave King, 12; Steve Lyne, 16, 18
Kimball Stock/Alan Robinson, 6, 8; Ron Kimball, cover
Peter Arnold/W. Layer, 14
Ulrike Schanz Photodesign & Animal Stock, 10